NOW IS NOT FOREVER

NOW IS NOT FOREVER

a grief journal of hope

Luan Louis

WESTBOW
PRESS
A DIVISION OF THOMAS NELSON

Westbow Press books may be ordered through booksellers or by contacting:

WestBow Press
A Division of Thomas Nelson
1663 Liberty Drive
Bloomington, IN 47403
www.westbowpress.com
1-(866) 928-1240

Because of the dynamic nature of the Internet, any Web addresses or links contained in this book may have changed since publication and may no longer be valid. The views expressed in this work are solely those of the author and do not necessarily reflect the views of the publisher, and the publisher hereby disclaims any responsibility for them.

Cover design:
©iStockphoto.com/Courtney Henschen
©iStockphoto.com/JJRD, ©iStockphoto.com/ArtisticCaptures,
©iStockphoto.com/pappamaart, ©iStockphoto.com/aniszewski,
©iStockphoto.com/DrPas

Special thanks to Courtney Henschen for designing the cover. www.CourtneyMaria.com

ISBN: 978-1-4497-1057-6 (sc)
ISBN: 978-1-4497-1058-3 (dj)
ISBN: 978-1-4497-1056-9 (e)

Library of Congress Control Number: 2010943076

Printed in the United States of America

WestBow Press rev. date: 1/10/2011

FOR JEFF

CONTENTS

PREFACE

When my husband of thirty-one years, Jeff Henschen, passed away in 2004, I held firmly to my anchor, Jesus Christ. He spoke to me very clearly in the days that followed, so I began to journal the comforting words that came to me daily in various ways. God knew exactly what I needed to hear, when I needed it, for as long as I needed it.

I long to share these words of comfort and encouragement with others who have lost a loved one. I urge you to listen as the Savior speaks to you and begin your personal journal in the lines provided.

He is the God who comforts, and He knows us each by name. I pray that He will use this journal to help you through your grief journey.

In Christ,
Luan Henschen Louis

"To all who mourn in [Christ], He will give beauty for ashes, joy instead of mourning, praise instead of despair."
Isaiah 61:3

Now is Not Forever

Because of His amazing grace,
I'll see my Savior face to face
When through death I leave this place
To start my new endeavor.

Because of His redeeming love
I'll rise to live with Him above,
Soaring as a peaceful dove;
We'll always be together.

Because He holds my future there,
There is no need for my despair.
A Heavenly home with Him I'll share;
For now is not forever.

Luan Louis

DAY ONE

"The Lord before whom I walk will send His angel with you and make your journey a success."
                                            Genesis 24:40a (NIV)

"Those who look to Him for help will be radiant with joy; no shadow of shame will darken their faces. I cried out to the Lord in my suffering and he heard me. He set me free from all my fears. For the angel of the Lord guards all who fear Him and rescues them."
                                            Psalm 34:5–7

"Taste and see that the Lord is good. Oh the joys of those who trust in Him!"
                                            Psalm 34:8

"I will hide beneath the shadow of your wings until this violent storm is past."
                                            Psalm 57:1b

"Jesus spoke . . . 'It's all right. I am here. Don't be afraid.'"
                                            Mark 6:50b

Write a prayer asking God to speak to you through the words in this journal.

_____

_____

_____

_____

_____

_____

_____

DAY TWO

Job undergoes a conversion in his mind and heart: from complaining about what he has lost to concentrating on what he is—a son of God. In the realization of his sonship he experiences the meaning of his existence; he discovers the meaning of life . . . God alone is good. Everything we have is a gift. The Lord gives and the Lord takes away . . . When we realize this, it is as though everything we lost comes back to us.
Richard Rohr and Joseph Martos

In the midst of my sorrow I must realize that I am still a child of the King.

We live by *trusting* in Him, not by the benefits, happiness, or success we may experience in this life. Our hope comes from God.
Bible study notes on book of Habakkuk

Time takes even the small and simple memories we hold of those we love and silently turns them into gold.

Your thoughts:

_____

_____

_____

_____

_____

_____

_____

_____

DAY THREE

The significant ways our loved one touched our lives cannot be diminished by death. The happiness we shared cannot be destroyed by grief. Time will fade our sorrow, but love is eternal.

"Trust God from the bottom of your heart; don't try to figure out everything on your own. Listen for God's voice in everything you do, everywhere you go; He's the one who will keep you on track."
Proverbs 3:5–6 (*The Message*)

Write a good memory of your loved one.

_____

_____

_____

_____

_____

_____

_____

_____

_____

_____

_____

_____

_____

_____

DAY FOUR

The stronger you love, the stronger you will grieve.

Some souls refresh us like a gentle shower. They touch our lives and return to Jesus—the Higher Power.

The life given us by nature is short, but the memory of a well-spent life is eternal.
                                        Cicero

What the heart has once owned and had, it shall never lose.
                              Henry Ward Beecher

Lord, help my special memories replace my sorrow with peace and joy.

We must never lose our faith or the thought of Jesus' face watching over us. He is the port in any storm.
                          2004 Sharing Our Faith devotional

Your thoughts:

_____

_____

_____

_____

_____

_____

_____

_____

DAY FIVE

The sun is gone now, but I'm not sad. Someone else is enjoying a sunrise.
2004 Sharing Our Faith devotional

My loved one is gone now, but I can be glad because Jesus is enjoying his/
her "rise" to Heaven.

The ones we love are never gone; they live within our hearts. The comfort
of memories will far outlast this sadness.

"Look straight ahead and fix your eyes on what lies before you. Mark out
a straight path for your feet; then stick to the path and stay safe."
Proverbs 4:25–26

"You keep track of all my sorrows. You have collected all my tears in your
bottle. You have recorded each one in your book."
Psalm 56:8

Jesus cares about you so very much!

Tell God about your sorrows today.

_____

_____

_____

_____

_____

_____

_____

_____

DAY SIX

As you hold me close in memory even though we are apart, my spirit
will live on, there within your heart …
I am with you always.
When you lean on trusted friends and their caring hugs enfold you,
within their loving arms I'll be there to hold you …
I am with you always.
And beyond the far horizon when we'll finally be together, where love
will be eternal and life will last forever …
I am with you always.

Lisa O. Engelhardt

"And be sure of this: I am with you always, even to the end of the age."
Matthew 28:20b

How do these words comfort you?

_____

_____

_____

_____

_____

_____

_____

_____

_____

_____

DAY SEVEN

Please don't sing sad songs for me,
Forget your grief and fears,
For I am in a perfect place,
Away from pain and tears....
I'm far away from hunger
And hurt and want and pride.
I have a place in Heaven
With the master by my side.
My life on earth was very good,
As earthly lives can go,
But paradise is so much more
Than anyone can know....
My heart is filled with happiness
And sweet rejoicing, too.
To walk with God is perfect peace,
A joy forever new.

Author Unknown

"You will keep in perfect peace all who trust in You, whose thoughts are fixed on you! Trust in the Lord always, for the Lord God is the eternal Rock."
Isaiah 26:3–4

Your thoughts:

_____

_____

_____

_____

_____

DAY EIGHT

"Yet we have this assurance: those who belong to God will live; their bodies will rise again."

Isaiah 26:19a

"But as for me, I know that my Redeemer lives, and that He will stand upon the earth at last. And after my body has decayed, yet in my body I will see God. I will see Him for myself. Yes I will see Him with my own eyes. I am overwhelmed at the thought!"

Job 19:25–27

"He will take these weak, mortal bodies of ours and change them into glorious bodies like His own, using the same mighty power that He will use to conquer everything, everywhere."

Philippians 3:21

What do you think Heaven will be like?

_____

_____

_____

_____

_____

_____

_____

_____

_____

_____

DAY NINE

"The Lord is my Shepherd;
I have everything I need.
He lets me rest in green meadows;
He leads me beside peaceful streams.
He renews my strength.
He guides me along right paths,
Bringing honor to His name.
Even when I walk
Through the dark valley of death,
I will not be afraid,
For you are close beside me.
Your rod and Your staff
Protect and comfort me.
You prepare a feast for me
In the presence of my enemies.
You welcome me as a guest anointing
My head with oil.
My cup overflows with blessings.
Surely Your goodness and unfailing love
Will pursue me all the days of my life
And I will dwell in the house of the Lord forever."
Psalm 23 (NLT)

My loved one is dwelling in the house of the Lord forever.

"Those who are wise will shine as bright as the sky, and those who turn many to righteousness will shine like stars forever."
Daniel 12:3

My loved one was a shining light to others.

"You will show me the way of life, granting me the joy of your presence and the pleasures of living with You forever."
Psalm 16:11

DAY TEN

"I have fought a good fight; I have finished the race, and I have remained faithful. And now the prize awaits me—the crown of righteousness that the Lord, the righteous Judge will give me on that great day of His return."
2 Timothy 4:7–8

"A single day in your courts is better than a thousand anywhere else!"
Psalm 84:10

"Sing loud praises to Him who rides the clouds."
Psalm 68:4

"Sing to the One who rides across the ancient Heavens."
Psalm 68:33

Write Psalm 100. (For your convenience, I have listed in the Appendix the Scriptures in these daily prompts.)

_____

_____

_____

_____

_____

_____

_____

_____

_____

_____

DAY ELEVEN

"You have allowed me to suffer much hardship, but you will restore me to life again and lift me up from the depths of the earth. You will restore me to even greater honor and comfort me once again."
Psalm 71:20–21

I will turn your mourning into joy; I will comfort you and give you gladness for sorrow.
Jeremiah 31:13b (paraphrased)

When a seed is planted in the earth, it disappears for a time—then it bursts forth with new life!

"So it will be with the resurrection … The body that is sown is perishable, it is raised imperishable."
1 Corinthians 15:42 (NIV)

Write Psalm 121:5.

_____

_____

_____

_____

_____

_____

_____

_____

_____

_____

DAY TWELVE

It's not in trying but in trusting;
Not in running but in resting;
It's not in wondering but in praying,
That we find the strength of the Lord.

Author Unknown

"Love never gives up, never loses faith, is always hopeful, and endures
through every circumstance. Love will last forever."
1 Corinthians 13:7-8a

A rose may lose its bloom, but still the fragrance lingers long.
A bird may fly away, yet we can still recall its song.
So when someone who is loved departs to join the Lord above,
They'll live and laugh and be with us in memories of love.

In His arms there is
Strength to hold you ...
Grace to sustain you ...
And love to carry you through.

DaySpring Cards

"The eternal God is thy refuge, and underneath are the everlasting
arms."
Deuteronomy 33:27(KJV)

Make a list of people who love you.

_____

_____

_____

DAY THIRTEEN

There is a peaceful place around the bend where your heart will see the sun's rays lift the fog of grief.

Compassionately …
May God's love heal your sorrow.
Affectionately …
May the prayers of friends be a sweet incense to the Father and thus ease your heartache.
Gently …
May your pain diminish as your fond, loving memories flourish.

As the caterpillar changes into a butterfly, so we will be transformed into glorious new bodies in Heaven.

List some ways God is encouraging you.

_____

_____

_____

_____

_____

_____

_____

_____

_____

_____

_____

DAY FOURTEEN

God, in His great mercy, knew when loved ones had to part;
Something special would be needed to bring comfort to the heart.
So He gave us each a precious gift not even time can fade,
Of reliving tender moments through the memories we've made.
It's so difficult to understand why loss must come to be.
But thank God for precious moments that live on in memory—
Of smiles exchanged and joys expressed
Of ups and downs you shared;
Of times you laughed together, and of all the ways you cared—
For when time has brought you comfort
Through its gentle healing touch,
Your most precious gifts will be those thoughts
Of the one you loved so much.

Emily Matthews, American Greetings

"May Your unfailing love be my comfort, according to Your promise."
Psalm 119:76 (NIV)

Your thoughts:

_____

_____

_____

_____

_____

_____

_____

_____

_____

DAY FIFTEEN

"But the fact is that Christ has been raised from the dead. He has become the first of a great harvest of those who will be raised to life again."
1 Corinthians 15:20

"Our bodies now disappoint us, but when they are raised, they will be full of glory. They are weak now, but when they are raised, they will be full of power. Every human being has an earthly body just like Adam's, but our heavenly bodies will be just like Christ's . . . How we thank God, who gives us victory over sin and death through Jesus Christ our Lord!"
1 Corinthians 15:43, 44, 48, 57

My loved one has the victory!
Christians never say good-bye to each other for the last time.

"And the God of all grace, who called you to His eternal glory in Christ, after you have suffered a little while, will Himself restore you and make you strong, firm and steadfast."
1 Peter 5:10–11 (NIV)

The power of God is released in our lives when we respond obediently to Him.
2004 Sharing Our Faith devotional

Say a prayer of thanks for God's power over death.

_____

_____

_____

_____

_____

_____

DAY SIXTEEN

RISING SON

Though troubles come
And sorrows abound …
The sun still rises.
When life seems tough
Like a turbulent flight …
The sun still rises.
While time here is short
And our loved ones pass on …
The sun still rises.
Thank God for His love
And the hope that He gives …
For the Son has risen!

Luan Louis

"God blesses the people who patiently endure testing. Afterward they will receive the crown of life that God has promised to those who love Him."
James 1:12
(This describes my loved one.)

Describe your loved one.

_____

_____

_____

_____

_____

DAY SEVENTEEN

"Don't be troubled. You trust God, now trust in me. There are many rooms in my Father's home, and I am going to prepare a place for you ... When everything is ready, I will come and get you, so that you will always be with me where I am."

John 14:1–3

Jesus *really* wanted my loved one to come be with Him!

God's will may come in stages. He may give us transition periods and times of waiting to help us depend on Him and trust His timing. If we patiently do His will during the transition times, we will be better prepared to serve Him as we should when He calls us.

Bible study notes on Genesis 11:31

I know that my Redeemer lives. There is no need to fear tomorrow because the future is in His hands. His love is unfailing!

Describe unfailing love.

_____

_____

_____

_____

_____

_____

_____

_____

_____

DAY EIGHTEEN

I have held many things in my hands, and I have lost them all; but whatever I have placed in God's hands, that I still possess.
Martin Luther

"He is the source of every mercy and the God who comforts us. He comforts us in all our troubles so that we can comfort others."
2 Corinthians 1:3b–4a

We are all made of "mud & water." If we would allow God's breathed Word to "ruffle us," He will shine His light on us, and use us to illuminate His nature, goodness, mercy and grace to all who stop "nodding off" and open their eyes.
2004 Sharing Our Faith devotional

"The Lord will work out His plans for my life—for your faithful love, O Lord, endures forever."
Psalm 138:8a

He will enable you as you depend on Him.
Joanie Yoder

But this precious treasure—this light and power that shone within my loved one—was held in a perishable container, that is, in his weak body. So everyone could see his glorious power was from God, and was not his own.
2 Corinthians 4:7 (paraphrased)

"Our hearts ache, but we always have joy."
2 Corinthians 6:10

There is true joy in *knowing* and serving Jesus.

DAY NINETEEN

I think that each one of us wants to look back on our lives and see that we have lived a life that counts. "Therefore since Christ suffered in His body, arm yourselves also with the same attitude, because he who has suffered in his body is done with sin. As a result, he does not live the rest of his earthly life for evil human desires, but rather for the will of God." (1 Peter 4:1–2 NIV)

A life that counts requires us first to enter into a personal relationship with Jesus Christ through faith. We saw Jeff live every day with tremendous faith in Jesus Christ—it was the strength of the relationship that motivated and sustained him.

The second thing we saw was that those areas of difficulty in Jeff's life were turned into his greatest ministry. He was able to speak with many, many people facing surgeries, illness, disease, and other difficulties—and comfort them as they faced the unknown—an area where he had lived most of his life.

And as the verse above says, he did not live his life for his own desires, but for the will of God.

Jeff finished well—a life that counts.

Mark Henschen

What goals can you set for yourself so you will be living a life that counts?

_____

_____

_____

_____

_____

_____

_____

DAY TWENTY

The legacy of love given and received remains behind to light the lives of those we touched along life's way ... each memory a beacon shining bright.

The dawn will bring another day, and with it the chance to be
A light in the life of others as you were a light to me.
In faith with hope and trust in God, I too, will try to be
A source of strength for others, in your loving memory.
Bee Ewing

"He who dwells in the shelter of the most high will rest in the shadow of the Almighty. I will say of the Lord, He is my refuge and my fortress, my God in whom I trust."
Psalm 91:1–2 (NIV)

This is not an ending but a new beginning of eternal life in our Father's Heavenly home.
DaySpring Cards

Life has sorrow ... and then we smile once more.

What makes you smile?

_____

_____

_____

_____

_____

_____

DAY TWENTY-ONE

"This is what I have asked of God for you: that you will be encouraged and knit together by strong ties of love, and that you will have the rich experience of knowing Christ with real certainty and clear understanding."
Colossians 2:2 (TLB)

Our family has been very closely knit together in love through this whole experience. I am so thankful to God for this and for helping us by showing each one of us different things we needed to see or hear to help us make it through.

"I will praise you O Lord my God, with all my heart; I will glorify your name forever."
Psalm 86:12 (NIV)

"And we know that all things work together for good to those who love God; to those who are the called according to His purpose."
Romans 8:28–29 (NKJV)

God's timing is always perfect!

Your thoughts:

_____

_____

_____

_____

_____

_____

_____

DAY TWENTY-TWO

"For we know that when this earthly tent we live in is taken down—when we die and leave these bodies—we will have a home in Heaven, an eternal body made for us by God Himself and not by human hands. We grow weary in our present bodies, and we long for the day when we will put on our heavenly bodies like new clothing. For we will not be spirits without bodies, but we will put on new heavenly bodies."
2 Corinthians 5:1–3

Christ died young, but His work was finished. We don't have to live a long life to do all that God has planned for us to do. Some of God's best servants have died at an early age—early from our standpoints—at the right time from God's. They, too, had finished the work God had for them to do.
Erwin W. Lutzer

God is peopling Heaven; why should he limit Himself to old people?
Jim Elliot

List some ways you can serve God.

_____

_____

_____

_____

_____

_____

_____

_____

_____

DAY TWENTY-THREE

When a stone is dropped into a lake, it quickly disappears from sight, but its impact leaves behind a series of ripples that broaden and reach across the water.

In the same way, the impact of one life lived for Christ will leave behind an influence for good that will reach the lives of many others.
Roy Lessin, DaySpring Cards

The testimony for Christ that your loved one has left behind will continue to reach out as a blessing to many other lives, just like it has been to mine.
DaySpring Cards

Father, I ask you to bless my friends and family. Show them a new revelation of your love and power. Holy Spirit, I ask you to minister to their spirit at this very moment. Where there is pain, give them your peace and mercy. Where there is self-doubt, release a renewed confidence through your grace.

If you know Jesus, you always have reasons to rejoice!

Write a prayer of thankfulness.

_____

_____

_____

_____

_____

_____

_____

_____

DAY TWENTY-FOUR

"He calls His own sheep by name and leads them out."
John 10:3b

You don't need to know where you're going if you are following the Shepherd.

God took that one. And in my lonely heart He poured His special peace, His tender love; I cannot doubt that God has drawn me near to trust Him more until I'm drawn above.
Morris

In every desert of trial, God has an oasis of comfort.
Dave Branon

"So don't be anxious about tomorrow. God will take care of your tomorrow, too. Live one day at a time."
Matthew 6:34 (TLB)

"May the Lord bring you into an even deeper understanding of the love of God and of the patience that comes from Christ."
2 Thessalonians 3:5 (TLB)

What concerns do you need to give to God?

_____

_____

_____

_____

_____

_____

DAY TWENTY-FIVE

Dear Heavenly Father, I thank and praise you for the signs and reminders you place in the sky. The star of Bethlehem, (the birth of your son, Jesus); the cross, (the crucifixion of Jesus); the rainbow, (your love for us); the sun, moon and stars, (You are the light of the world).
2004 Sharing Our Faith devotional

"Be still and know that I am God."
Psalm 46:10a (NIV)

A mighty power resides in silence. When a crisis strikes, we need to find some quiet moments, an interval away from the confusion and noise about us. Then we can hear the still, small voice of God calling us to restoration and wholeness.

Only when the winds and storms of the world that blow across our lives are quieted can we catch and reflect the beauty of the Infinite.
Henry Gariepy

Spend some time in quiet reflection.

_____

_____

_____

_____

_____

_____

_____

_____

_____

DAY TWENTY-SIX

God is in control of every situation no matter how hard it may be to go through.

"If we are living now by the Holy Spirit, let us follow the Holy Spirit's leading in *every* part of our lives."
Galatians 5:25

As we live by the Holy Spirit's power, we need to submit every aspect of our life to God: emotional, physical, social, intellectual, vocational.
Because we are sons and daughters, we have His Holy Spirit as the loving guarantee of His approval. Use your freedom to live for Christ and serve Him as He desires.
Bible study notes on Galatians 5–6

"The righteous cry out and the Lord hears them; He delivers them from all their troubles. The Lord is close to the brokenhearted and saves those who are crushed in spirit."
Psalm 34:17–18 (NIV)

Learn to commit all your feelings to the Lord. He understands and cares.

Write a note to Jesus telling how you feel.

_____

_____

_____

_____

_____

_____

DAY TWENTY-SEVEN

"I wait quietly before God, for my hope is in Him. He alone is my rock and my salvation, my fortress where I will not be shaken."
Psalm 62:5–6

"My heart has heard you say, 'Come and talk with me.' And my heart responds, 'Lord I am coming.'"
Psalm 27:8

God delights in my prayers and time with Him.

"Do not be anxious about anything, but in everything, by prayer and petition, with thanksgiving, present your requests to God. And the peace of God, which transcends all understanding, will guard your hearts and your minds in Christ Jesus."
Philippians 4:6–7 (NIV)

What worries can you pray about today?

_____

_____

_____

_____

_____

_____

_____

_____

_____

_____

DAY TWENTY-EIGHT

Happiness is something you choose. Whether you like your life or not doesn't depend on how it's arranged. It is how you arrange your mind. Remind yourself often of all that Jesus has given to you and be thankful. That is how to arrange your mind.

David Roper

"Fix your thoughts on what is true and honorable and right. Think about things that are pure and lovely and admirable. Think about things that are excellent and worthy of praise ... and the God of peace will be with you."

Philippians 4:8b, 9b

The symphony of a life well lived echoes through time. If we listen, the music plays on in a loving refrain.

"Show me your ways, O Lord, teach me your paths; guide me in your truth and teach me, for you are my God my Savior, and my hope is in you all day long.

Psalm 25:4–5 (NIV)

How has God blessed you this week?

_____

_____

_____

_____

_____

_____

_____

DAY TWENTY-NINE

Speak and live and love with purpose so there will be no regrets.

"[B]ut those who hope in the Lord will renew their strength. They will soar on wings like eagles; they will run and not grow weary, they will walk and not be faint."
Isaiah 40:31 (NIV)

"On my bed I remember you; I think of you through the watches of the night. Because you are my help, I sing in the shadow of your wings. I stay close to you; your right hand upholds me."
Psalm 63:6–7 (NIV)

"What joy for those you choose to bring near, those who live in your holy courts. What joy awaits us inside your holy temple!"
Psalm 65:4

Your thoughts:

_____

_____

_____

_____

_____

_____

_____

_____

_____

_____

DAY THIRTY

God sees through your tears to comfort the pain and sorrow of your heart. You may still often feel lonely, but you will never be alone.

"'I will never fail you, I will never forsake you' says the Lord."
Hebrews 13:5b

"For the Lord your God goes with you; He will never leave you or forsake you."
Deuteronomy 31:6b (NIV)

"Casting all your cares on Him, for He cares for you."
1 Peter 5:7 (NKJV)

"I am overcome with joy because of your unfailing love, for you have seen my troubles and you care about the anguish of my soul."
Psalm 31:7

For the child of God, death is the gateway to glory.

Thank God for His promise to always be with you.

_____

_____

_____

_____

_____

_____

_____

DAY THIRTY-ONE

"For the troubles we see will soon be over, but the joys to come will last forever."

2 Corinthians 4:18b

My loved one is already receiving his "joys to come."

All souls will pass from this earth, but their memories live on in the hearts of those who loved them.

Sometimes words cannot express sentiments as well as thoughtful silences, softly whispering of caring.

Death separates us for a time; Christ will reunite us forever.

Dave Branon

"I know the plans I have for you, declares the Lord, plans to prosper you and not to harm you; plans to give you hope and a future."

Jeremiah 29:11 (NIV)

Your thoughts:

_____

_____

_____

_____

_____

_____

_____

_____

_____

DAY THIRTY-TWO

"Jesus said, 'I tell you the truth, whoever hears my word and believes Him who sent me has eternal life, and will not be condemned; he has crossed over from death to life.'"
John 5:24 (NIV)

My loved one has crossed over from death to life.
We are never really apart because he is a part of me.

"Whatever happens, dear brothers and sisters, may the Lord give you joy."
Philippians 3:1

"But our citizenship is in Heaven. And we eagerly await a Savior from there, the Lord Jesus Christ, who, by the power that enables him to bring everything under his control, will transform our lowly bodies so that they will be like his glorious body."
Philippians 3:20–21 (NIV)

What do you think our new, glorious bodies will be like?

_____

_____

_____

_____

_____

_____

_____

_____

DAY THIRTY-THREE

"Don't worry about anything; instead, pray about everything. Tell God what you need and thank Him for all He has done. If you do this, you will experience God's peace which is far more wonderful than the human mind can understand. His peace will guard your hearts and minds as you live in Christ Jesus."

Philippians 4:6–7

Whenever you start to worry, stop and pray. Let God's peace guard your heart against anxiety.

Bible study notes on Philippians 4:6–7

I got up this morning to a beautiful, sunny sky, and I was so happy and thankful. But not even an hour later, the clouds had rolled in, and it was an overcast sky. I immediately began grumbling. But when I went outside, I noticed the birds were still singing their cheerful songs.

We can learn a lesson from the springtime birds. Whether it's a sunny morning or a cloudy one, they keep singing their songs of praise to the Creator.

"Always be full of joy in the Lord. I say it again, rejoice!"

Philippians 4:4

Your thoughts:

_____

_____

_____

_____

_____

_____

DAY THIRTY-FOUR

When we've been there ten-thousand years,
Bright shining as the sun,
We've no less days to sing God's praise
Than when we first begun.

John Newton

When our dreams are shattered and our hearts are broken, we may feel
that all has been lost and nothing has been gained. It takes the touch of
God to open our eyes to the greater glory of His plan.
David McCasland

Only when we are looking for Jesus in our midst will we experience the
power and help He can bring.
Bible study notes on Luke 24:13ff

"You will show me the path of life; in Your presence is fullness of joy; at
Your right hand are pleasures forevermore."
Psalm 16:11 (NKJV)

Write some words from your favorite hymn or chorus.

_____

_____

_____

_____

_____

_____

_____

DAY THIRTY-FIVE

"[G]et to know the God of your ancestors. Worship and serve Him with your whole heart and with a willing mind. For the Lord sees every heart and understands and knows every plan and thought. If you seek Him you will find Him."

1 Chronicles 28:9

"Happy are those who obey His decrees and search for Him with all their hearts."

Psalm 119:2

"He rewards those who sincerely seek Him."

Hebrews 11:6c

Jesus is within reach of all who will look to Him and touch Him with the hand of faith.

Mart DeHaan

"I lift up my eyes to the hills—where does my help come from? My help comes from the Lord, the maker of Heaven and Earth."

Psalm 121:1–2 (NIV)

Write your favorite Bible verse.

_____

_____

_____

_____

_____

_____

DAY THIRTY-SIX

"Before they call I will answer; while they are still speaking I will hear."
Isaiah 65:24 (NIV)

Thank you, Lord, for listening and having an understanding heart.

O Divine Master, grant that I may not so much seek to be consoled, as to console; to be understood, as to understand; to be loved, as to love. For it is in giving that we receive; it is in pardoning that we are pardoned; and it is in dying that we are born to eternal life.
Francis of Assisi

From me to my loved one:
"For though I am far away from you, my heart is with you. And I am very happy because you are *living* "emphasis mine" [in Heaven] as you should and because of your strong faith in Christ."
Colossians 2:5

Write a message from you to your loved one.

_____

_____

_____

_____

_____

_____

_____

_____

_____

_____

DAY THIRTY-SEVEN

"Since you have been raised to new life with Christ, set your sights on the realities of Heaven, where Christ sits at God's right hand in the place of honor and power. Let Heaven fill your thoughts …"
Colossians 3:1–2a

"Devote yourselves to prayer with an alert mind and a thankful heart."
Colossians 4:2

Beautiful character begins in the heart.
David McCasland

Experiencing problems and persecutions can build character (James 1:3–4), perseverance (Rom. 5:3–5), and sensitivity toward others who also face troubles (2 Cor. 1:3–7).

This is the ministry God gave to my loved one. And he finished his assignment—his mission.

How can you minister to others today?

_____

_____

_____

_____

_____

_____

_____

_____

_____

DAY THIRTY-EIGHT

My Lord is ever with me along life's busy way;
I'll trust in Him completely for guidance day by day.
Anonymous

"Show me where to walk, for I have come to you in prayer."
Psalm 143:8b

Christ's return is more than a doctrine, it is a promise. It is not just for the future; it has a vital impact on how we live now.
Bible study notes on 2 Thessalonians 3:18

"Forgetting what is behind and straining toward what is ahead, I press on toward the goal to win the prize for which God has called me heavenward in Christ Jesus."
Philippians 3:13–14 (NIV)

"But we are citizens of heaven, where the Lord Jesus Christ lives."
Philippians 3:20

My loved one no longer has a weak, mortal body, but a glorious one!

Your thoughts:

_____

_____

_____

_____

_____

_____

DAY THIRTY-NINE

A Prayer for Light

Jesus, light of the world, when I am afraid and unsure,
Comfort me with the light of Your presence.
When loneliness chills me, warm me with the light of Your love.
When the road ahead seems dark, guide me with the light of Your way.
When I don't understand and my thoughts are unclear, fill me with
the Light of Your wisdom. When I seem spent like a candle consumed,
Replenish me with the light of Your life.
Then, so filled with Your light, use me, so that I, with You, may be Light
for the world.

Wally Hyclak

Dwell not on the past—only on the present. So store only the blessings from the Lord, the Light of the world. Encourage yourself by the thought of these. Bury your disappointments and go forward to a new and risen life. And for each day, God will supply the wisdom and the strength. Once you are born of the Spirit, *that* is your life's breath. How often does God go before you to prepare the way, to soften a heart here, to over-rule there.
from *God Calling*

Ask God to replenish you with His love.

_____

_____

_____

_____

_____

_____

DAY FORTY

Springtime is wonderful, God; the sunshine, the warm breezes, the flowers and grass breaking through the ground. How refreshing to know that life can have a new start; that what seems like the end of things is really a beginning. Thanks for showing us that our mistakes can be forgiven and we can be made new just like flowers and grass in springtime.

Marilyn Jansen

"Then I heard every creature in Heaven and on earth and under the earth and on the sea, and all that is in them singing: 'To Him who sits on the throne and to the Lamb be praise and honor and glory and power, forever and ever!'"

Revelation 5:13 (NIV)

"So be truly glad! There is wonderful joy ahead. For God has reserved a priceless inheritance for His children … and your faith is far more precious to God than mere gold. It is all so wonderful that even the angels are eagerly watching these things happen."

from 1 Peter 1:6, 4, 7, 12

Your thoughts:

_____

_____

_____

_____

_____

_____

_____

_____

_____

DAY FORTY-ONE

"O lord, you saw me before I was born and scheduled each day of my life before I began to breathe. Every day was recorded in your book."
Psalm 139:16 (TLB)

We must honor our departed loved ones by holding on to God's hand. We don't understand, but we still must trust God as we await the great reunion He has planned for us.
Dave Branon

Though tragedy, heartache, and sorrow abound,
And many a hardship in life will be found,
I'll put all my trust in the Savior of light,
For He can bring hope in the darkest of night.
D. DeHaan

"Oh how kind and gracious the Lord was! He filled me completely with faith and the love of Christ Jesus."
1 Timothy 1:14

Pray that God will help your faith remain strong through this time.

_____

_____

_____

_____

_____

_____

_____

_____

DAY FORTY-TWO

"O Lord, you have examined my heart and know everything about me. You know when I sit down or stand up. You know my every thought when far away. You chart the path ahead of me and tell me where to stop and rest. Every moment you know where I am. You know what I am going to say even before I say it, Lord. You both precede and follow me. You place your hand of blessing on my head . . . Search me Oh God and know my heart; test me and know my thoughts. Point out anything in me that offends you, and lead me along the path of everlasting life."

Psalm 139:1–5, 23–24

Your life is so linked up with those of others, so bound by circumstances that to let your desire have instant fulfillment might in many cases cause another, as earnest prayer, to go unanswered.

Delay is not denial. It is the opportunity for God to work out your problems and accomplish your desires in the most wonderful way possible for you. Oh! Child, trust me.

from *God Calling*

What specific thing do you need to trust Him for today?

DAY FORTY-THREE

You and I are not the source of light that enlightens the world. We can only receive the oil of the Holy Spirit that fuels the living flame He produces. If we burn steadily through the long, dark hours, it is because we have learned to yield our lives to the Spirit's unlimited supply of power and strength. This comes only through continual fellowship with Jesus our Savior.

It is not what we do for the Lord, but what *He* does *through* us that enlightens and enriches others. We must be satisfied to be a bright and shining lamp, drawing from the hidden resources of the indwelling Spirit of Christ. Our role is to help others see the glory of His light.

David Roper

My loved one was a beacon of light to others.

Time is:
Too slow for those who wait; too swift for those who fear;
Too long for those who grieve; too short for those who rejoice;
But for those who love,
Time is not.

Henry VanDyke

Your thoughts:

_____

_____

_____

_____

_____

_____

DAY FORTY-FOUR

If God is going to do His deepest work in you, it will begin with surrender. So give it all to God: your past regrets, your present problems, your future ambitions, your fears, dreams, weaknesses, habits, hurts, and hang-ups. Put Jesus Christ in the driver's seat of your life and take your hands off the steering wheel. Don't be afraid. Nothing under His control can ever be out of control. Mastered by Christ, you can handle anything.
Rick Warren

"I can do all things through Christ who strengthens me."
Philippians 4:13 (NKJV)

Delight in God's love. Try to live in the rapture of the kingdom. Joy in Him, trust in Him, share all of life with Him; see Him in everything; rejoice in Him. And give Him the joy of sharing all with you.
from *God Calling*

Write a prayer of praise to God.

_____

_____

_____

_____

_____

_____

_____

_____

_____

_____

_____

DAY FORTY-FIVE

Leave more and more the choice to Christ. You will have no regrets.
from *God Calling*

"God has reserved a priceless inheritance for His children. It is kept in Heaven for you, pure and undefiled, beyond the reach of change and decay."
1 Peter 1:4

My loved one has reached his priceless inheritance.

When you have a relationship with God through Jesus, you don't need to fear death. It is the door to eternity. It will be the last hour of your time on earth, but it won't be the last of you. Rather than being the end of your life, it will be your birthday into eternal life. Hope is as essential to your life as air and water. You need hope to cope.
Rick Warren

I lead you. The way is clear. Go forward unafraid. I am beside you. Listen, listen, listen to my voice. My hand is controlling all.
from *God Calling*

Your thoughts:

_____

_____

_____

_____

_____

_____

DAY FORTY-SIX

As Jesus stepped into the garden, you were in His prayers. As Jesus looked into Heaven, you were in His vision. As Jesus dreamed of the day when we will be where He is, He saw you there. His final prayer was about you. His final pain was for you. His final passion was you.
Max Lucado

"Therefore, we who have fled to Him for refuge can take new courage, for we can hold onto His promise with confidence. This confidence is like a strong and trustworthy anchor for our souls."
Hebrews 6:18b–19a

Our hope is secure and immovable, anchored in God just as a ship's anchor holds firmly to the seabed.
Bible study notes on Hebrew 6:18–19

"You knew you had better things waiting for you in eternity."
Hebrews 10:34b

My loved one definitely has better things in eternity.

List things that will be better in Heaven.

_____

_____

_____

_____

_____

_____

_____

DAY FORTY-SEVEN

When suffering or confusion obscures our views of God, we can be honest with others about our doubts. But we can also express our confidence that the Lord is still there by recalling times we have witnessed His grandeur and goodness.

Julie Ackerman Link

God gives me wings to rise above
The clouds of trial that block the sun,
To soar above gray skies and see
The love and goodness of your Son.

Sper

"[P]ut into action God's saving work in your lives . . . For God is working in you, giving you the desire to obey Him and the power to do what pleases Him . . . Let your lives shine brightly ..."

Philippians 2:12b, 13, 15b

If the encouragement of our example helps another person to flourish and be successful, we should rejoice.

David McCasland

I rejoice that my loved one's example helped me and many others. I want to live up to and continue his ministry of encouragement.

How can you be an encouragement to others?

_____

_____

_____

_____

_____

DAY FORTY-EIGHT

What greater treasures can you have than peace and rest and joy? Joy, peace, love; God's great gifts. Follow Christ to find all three. Feel the thrill of protection and safety. Any soul can feel this in a harbor, but real joy and victory come to those alone who sense these when they ride a storm.

from *God Calling*

"All these faithful ones died without receiving what God had promised them, but they saw it all from a distance and welcomed the promises of God."

Hebrews 11:13

They saw the "big picture." My loved one saw the "big picture" and is now enjoying the Heavenly city.

Can you look beyond right now and see what might be in God's "big picture" for you?

_____

_____

_____

_____

_____

_____

_____

_____

_____

_____

_____

DAY FORTY-NINE

When it's cold on earth, we can take comfort in knowing that our loved ones are in the warm arms of God. And when Christ comes, we'll hold them too.

Max Lucado

May the arms that welcomed your loved one into Heaven be the same arms that hold your heart today.

DaySpring Cards

God, I give myself to you. Mold me into what you would have me be. I am merely a vessel shaped by the Master. Make me willing to be transformed. Use me where you need me. In all that I do, let me reflect the mastery of Your hands.

Marilyn Jansen

"Satisfy us in the morning with your unfailing love, that we may sing with joy and be glad all our days."

Psalm 90:14 (NIV)

Close your eyes and feel the arms of Jesus holding you.

_____

_____

_____

_____

_____

_____

_____

_____

DAY FIFTY

Only as the result of frequent converse with Jesus, of much prayer to Him, of listening to and obedience to His behests comes that intimacy that makes His followers dare to approach Him as friend to friend.

Ask not only the big things He has told you, but ask the little tender signs of love. Never think of Christ's love as only a tender compassion and forgiveness. It is that, but it is also the love of a lover who shows His love by countless words and actions and by tender thought.

from *God Calling*

What can I say to you? Your heart is torn. Then remember "He bindeth up the broken hearts". Just feel the tenderness of My hands as I bind up your wounds.

from *God Calling*

Thank you, God, for knowing us so well. When our little problems seem too tiny to bring to you, remind us that you care about every aspect of our lives. When the little things grow and become really big problems, remind us that we can cast all our cares on you—the little things and the big ones.

Marilyn Jansen

Write Hebrews 10:23.

DAY FIFTY-ONE

Never weary in prayer. When one day man sees how marvelously his prayer has been answered, then he will deeply, so deeply, regret that he prayed so little. Only in that earnest supplication, and the calm trust that results does man learn strength and gain peace.

from *God Calling*

A Christian's life is a window through which others can see Jesus.

Joanie Yoder

My loved one's life was like that.

"Sorrow may endure for a night but joy comes in the morning." My bravest are those who can anticipate the morning and feel "in the night of sorrow" that underlying joy that tells of confident expectations of the morning.

from *God Calling*

What is your prayer request today?

_____

_____

_____

_____

_____

_____

_____

_____

_____

_____

_____

DAY FIFTY-TWO

Life, eternal life is yours—revitalizing, renewing. Doubt flees, joy resigns and hope conquers!

from *God Calling*

Day by day and with each passing moment,
Strength I find to meet my trials here;
Trusting in my Father's wise bestowment,
I've no cause for worry or for fear.

Berg

Each day brings new reasons to pray to God, to praise His name, and to proclaim His love. Make your worship of Him something you do "from day to day."

Dave Branon

"I waited patiently for the Lord to help me, and He turned to me and heard my cry. He lifted me out of the pit of despair. He set my feet on solid ground and steadied me as I walked along. He has given me a new song to sing, a hymn of praise to our God. Oh the joys of those who trust the Lord! . . . My only hope is in your unfailing love and faithfulness."

Psalm 40:1–4a and 11b

Thank God for being constant and unchangeable even through your life changing experience.

DAY FIFTY-THREE

We must do the thing commanded—preach the gospel—and we must trust God for the results. If we wait until we are sure we will do a thing purely and perfectly, we shall never accomplish the will of God on earth.

Elisabeth Elliot

If the Lord be with us, we have no cause of fear. His eye is upon us, His arm over us, His ear open to our prayer—His grace sufficient, His promise unchangeable.

John Newton

"I will fear no evil, for thou art with me."

Psalm 23:4 (KJV)

"So I pray that God, who gives you hope, will keep you happy and full of peace as you believe in Him. May you overflow with hope through the power of the Holy Spirit."

Romans 15:13

In our dark world, God is light. In our cold world, God brings the warmth of love. In our dying world, God brings life. When we lack confidence, these truths bring us certainty.

from introductory Bible study notes on 1 John

Your thoughts:

_____

_____

_____

_____

_____

_____

DAY FIFTY-FOUR

By faith we acknowledge Christ as our Captain, Savior, Leader and Lord.
We come as we are so that we can become what He wants us to be.
David McCasland

"Father, I want these whom you have given me to be with me so they can
see my glory."
John 17:24a

When my loved one died, he left his body and entered the presence of His
Savior, where he beholds His glory.

The death of people whom we love brings sorrow and deep pain;
But if our loved ones know the Lord, Our loss becomes their gain.
Sper

When Christians die, they have just begun to live.
Herb Vander Lugt

Every day we live is a priceless gift of God, loaded with possibilities to learn
something new, to gain fresh insights into His great truths.
Dale Evans Rogers

Pray that God will give you wisdom as you face the future.

_____

_____

_____

_____

_____

_____

DAY FIFTY-FIVE

"The path of the righteous is like the first gleam of dawn, shining ever brighter till the full light of day."
Proverbs 4:18 (NIV)

"Mary sat at the Lord's feet listening to what He taught.… There is really only one thing worth being concerned about. Mary has discovered it."
Luke 10:39 and 42

Be thankful that there is One who knows; One who marks every crisis, every effort, every heartache. Abundance is God's supply. Receive showers of blessing and in your turn—shower!
from *God Calling*

Job listened, gave up his complaining, and found peace in surrendering to God. When troubles come and we complain because we do not understand, the problem is our narrow view that fails to see God's loving hand.
Mart and K. DeHaan

"But I am trusting you, O Lord, saying, 'You are my God!' My future is in your hands."
Psalm 31:14–15a

Your thoughts:

_____

_____

_____

_____

_____

_____

DAY FIFTY-SIX

Meeting every situation with thanksgiving isn't a denial of trouble. It helps us see those situations from God's perspective—as opportunities to discover His power and love.

Joanie Yoder

"But you dear friends must continue to build your lives on the foundation of your Holy Faith. And continue to pray as you are directed by the Holy Spirit. Live in such a way that God's love can bless you as you wait for the eternal life that our Lord Jesus Christ in His mercy is going to give you. All glory to God, who is able to keep you from stumbling, and who will bring you into His glorious presence innocent of sin and with great joy."

Jude 20, 21, 24

How wonderful to be in Jesus' presence and see Him face to face! And my loved one is already there!

Write what you are thankful for today.

_____

_____

_____

_____

_____

_____

_____

_____

_____

_____

DAY FIFTY-SEVEN

My Lord, You have heard the cry of my heart because it was you who cried out within my heart.

Thomas Merton

"And the God of all grace, who called you to His eternal glory in Christ, after you have suffered a little while, will Himself restore you and make you strong, firm and steadfast."

1 Peter 5:10 (NIV)

"May the God of hope fill you with all joy and peace as you trust in Him, so that you may overflow with hope by the power of the Holy Spirit."

Romans 15:13 (NIV)

A great love knows that in every difficulty, every trial, every failure, the presence of the loved one suffices. Test your love for Christ by this. Breathe in the rich blessings of each new day—forget all that lies behind you. Man is made that he can carry the weight of twenty-four hours—no more.

from *God Calling*

Live one day at a time.

Pray that Jesus will help you focus on Him today.

_____

_____

_____

_____

_____

_____

DAY FIFTY-EIGHT

"And the Holy Spirit helps us in our distress. For we don't even know what we should pray for, nor how we should pray. But the Holy Spirit prays for us with groanings that cannot be expressed in words. And the father who knows all hearts knows what the Spirit is saying, for the Spirit pleads for us believers in harmony with God's own will. And we know that God causes everything to work together for the good of those who love God and are called according to His purpose for them."
Romans 8:26–28

Thou best of Consolers, sweet guest of the soul, sweet refreshment. In labor, Thou art rest; in heat, the tempering; in grief, the consolation.
Hymn by unknown composer

"And I will ask the Father, and He will give you another Counselor [encourager, comforter], who will never leave you. He is the Holy Spirit who leads into all truth."
John 14:16–17a

Spend some time in silence and let the Holy Spirit speak on your behalf.

_____

_____

_____

_____

_____

_____

_____

_____

_____

DAY FIFTY-NINE

The Spirit lives within each Christian bringing the peace of Christ along with encouragement and alleviation of grief. The "sweet guest of the soul" is always with us on any day we remember our loved ones who have died. In grief, the Spirit is our consolation, the Light of our hearts, the giver of everlasting joy.

David McCasland

But to those who hear Christ's words and understand the Spirit's power, the Spirit gives a whole new way to look at life. We don't have to know the future to have faith in God; we have to have faith in God to be secure about the future.

Bible study notes on John 14:17–21

There is power in a prayer of praise. It keeps our focus on Jesus instead of our problems and opens our minds to all God has in store for our future.

"In your hands are strength and power to exalt and give strength to all. Now, our God, we give you thanks and praise your glorious name."

1 Chronicles 29:12b-13 (NIV)

Your thoughts:

_____

_____

_____

_____

_____

_____

_____

DAY SIXTY

The way of the soul's transformation is the way of divine companionship. Not so much the asking God to make you this or that, but the living with Him, thinking of Him, talking to Him—thus you grow like Him.

from *God Calling*

You are Christ's and will grow more like Him, your Master. The self, the original person, shrivels up and dies, and upon the soul becomes stamped Christ's image.

from *God Calling*

You must be faithful to Christ in your sufferings or sadness. Only then will your faith prove to be genuine.

Bible study notes on Revelation 2:10

"Everyone who is victorious will eat from the tree of life in the paradise of God."

Revelation 2:7b

How has God helped you be victorious?

_____

_____

_____

_____

_____

_____

_____

_____

DAY SIXTY-ONE

Live every moment for Christ and be prepared to meet Him today.
David McCasland

Drive fear and depression and a sense of failure out with praise. Do this until at last a thrill of joy, of thankful awe, will accompany the spoken word.
from *God Calling*

So on and up. Forward. Patience—perseverance—struggle. Remember that Christ is beside you, your Captain and your Helper.
from *God Calling*

Worship God and praise Him for what He has done, what He is doing, and what He will do for all who trust in Him. When we realize the glorious future that awaits us, we will find the strength to face our present difficulties.
Bible study notes on Revelation 5:9–10

We may be separated from our loved ones by distance, but they remain in our hearts.

Ask God to fill you with His praise instead of your despair.

_____

_____

_____

_____

_____

_____

_____

DAY SIXTY-TWO

Listen to My voice. Listen and you will never be disappointed. Listen and anxious thoughts and tired nerves will become rested. The tenderness and the restfulness will heal your scars and make you strong. Then let all your power be My power.

from God Calling

It is necessary that you see Christ as supplying all that you personally need. The weak need His strength. The strong need His tenderness. The lonely need a friend. No man could be all these to men—only God could.

from God Calling

My joy will suffice to heal all your sores and wounds. Trust me, love me and call upon me. Obtain me—your soul's joy and haven. Over and on and up. I am your Leader and your goal.

from God Calling

I have scars to show my failing, and the wrong turns that I took.
Only God did not forsake me, though the very mountains shook
And when my days are over, and all the shadows dim,
I'll close my eyes, take my Saviors hand, and leave the rest to Him.
Betty Jane Pukis

Write Psalm 34:7.

_____

_____

_____

_____

_____

_____

DAY SIXTY-THREE

Twilight Reflections
When I look up to the sky and see the twinkling stars above,
I might feel all alone here but I know the Father's love.
The vastness of the heavens may make me seem quite small,
But with Jesus in my heart I know the maker of it all.
He sees me when I falter on this new path I must trod,
So I continue onward as I hold the hand of God.
He's the Rock I lean on; He's my hope along this trail.
Jesus is my answer and I know He will not fail.
Luan Louis

Not only live, but grow in grace and power and beauty—the true beauty, the beauty of holiness. Reach ever forward after the things of God's Kingdom. So reaching after the treasures of His Kingdom your whole nature becomes changed so you can best enjoy and receive the wonders of that Kingdom.

from *God Calling*

"There is a time for everything, a season for every activity under Heaven. A time to be born and a time to die. A time to plant and a time to harvest . . . A time to cry and a time to laugh. A time to grieve and a time to dance."
Ecclesiastes 3:1, 2, 4

What character traits can help you become more like the people of the Kingdom of God?

_____

_____

_____

_____

_____

DAY SIXTY-FOUR

The Traveler

As I journey thru this desert
Of endless, barren dunes,
What I know, and how I feel
Are two discordant tunes.

I know that my Redeemer lives
And stays close by my side.
I feel a lonely wanderer
Amidst this sandstorm's tide.

Do you hear me, Jesus?
Do you know my heart's desire?
Have you seen me struggle, yearning
For that goal that I aspire?

"Yes," He gently chides me
As the moon winks thru the clouds.
"But you must learn to trust My way,
My choice, My time, My power.

"Let Me teach you how to be
More like Me as we walk.
Focus on Me. Listen to My words
Before you talk.

"You will grow in grace
As we traverse this sea of sand,
And as My will unfolds
You will finally understand."

Luan Louis

"[W]hen I sit in darkness, the Lord will be a light to me."
Micah 7:8 (NKJV)

DAY SIXTY-FIVE

"But those who wait on the Lord will find new strength. They will fly high on wings like eagles. They will run and not grow weary. They will walk and not faint."

Isaiah 40:31

It's an incredible blessing to have the Creator and Sustainer of our universe as a friend. Although worshiped by countless heavenly hosts, He takes great joy in His relationship with us.

Vernon Grounds

We are called to live each day with self discipline and spiritual discernment. We need to ask the Lord for His help so that we will see situations through His eyes and make wise choices. As we obey Him and stay within His limits, we will find true joy and lasting satisfaction.

Dave Egner

Your thoughts:

_____

_____

_____

_____

_____

_____

_____

_____

_____

_____

DAY SIXTY-SIX

To know that peace is to have received the stamp of the Kingdom—the mark of the Lord Jesus Christ. That peace is loving faith at rest.

from *God Calling*

"I know the Lord is always with me. I will not be shaken, for He is right beside me. No wonder my heart is filled with joy, and my mouth shouts His praises!"

Psalm 16:8–9a

"Without wavering, let us hold tightly to the hope we say we have, for God can be trusted to keep His promise … You knew you had better things waiting for you in eternity."

Hebrews 10:23, 34b

My loved one held onto the Hope and knew better things awaited him.

What do you hope for today?

_____

_____

_____

_____

_____

_____

_____

_____

_____

_____

_____

DAY SIXTY-SEVEN

Obedience is your great sign of faith. The secure, steadfast, immovable life of my disciples, the Rock Home, is not built at a wish in a moment, but is laid stone by stone, foundations, walls, roof, by acts of obedience, the daily following out of my wishes, the loving doing of my will. It is *there* I come to dwell with my loved one.

from *God Calling*

Death for us is not a dark journey into the unknown. It is not a lonely walk into a strange and friendless place. Rather, it is a glorious transition from the trials of earth into the joys of Heaven, where we will be reunited with our loved ones in Christ who have gone before. Best of all, we will enjoy the presence of our Lord forever!

Richard DeHaan

"For we know that when this earthly tent we live in is taken down—when we die and leave these bodies—we will have a home in Heaven, an eternal body made for us by God Himself and not by human hands."

2 Corinthians 5:1

Your thoughts:

_____

_____

_____

_____

_____

_____

_____

_____

DAY SIXTY-EIGHT

Praying, resting, waiting, trusting—these are words that tell a story; as we wait for God to lead us, He responds, "Just seek my glory."
Hess

Trees endure because they have roots that tap deep into the soil. They draw strength and nourishment from hidden subterranean sources. And so it is with us. Our ability to endure—no, to flourish—is dependent on our being rooted in Christ. Those who read His Word, reflect on it and pray it into their lives bring forth the fruit of the Spirit, even into old age.
David Roper

"And I pray that Christ will be more at home in your hearts as you trust in Him. May your roots go down deep into the soil of God's marvelous love."
Ephesians 3:17

"It is good to give thanks to the Lord, to sing praises to the most High!"
Psalm 92:1

Write Psalm 42:11.

_____

_____

_____

_____

_____

_____

_____

DAY SIXTY-NINE

Jesus—the name banishes loneliness—dispels gloom. Jesus—use it more. Use it tenderly. Use it prayerfully. Use it powerfully. Walk in My way and trust Me. I am yours as truly as you are mine. Rest in that truth.

from *God Calling*

"But if we are living in the light of God's presence, just as Christ is, then we have fellowship with each other, and the blood of Jesus, His Son, cleanses us from every sin."

1 John 1:7

Live in the Light of God's presence!

Fear not, I am with thee—O be not dismayed;
For I am thy God, I will still give thee aid.
I'll strengthen thee, help thee, and cause thee to stand,
Upheld by my gracious omnipotent hand.

Keith

Pray the name of Jesus over and over.

_____

_____

_____

_____

_____

_____

_____

_____

DAY SEVENTY

Lord, why should I doubt any more, when you have given me such assured pledges of your love? First, you are my Creator, I your creature; you my Master, I your servant. You are my Father, I your child.
Anne Bradstreet

Sometimes, God, the path before me is difficult. But help me do my best in walking it. When I am tired, give me energy. When I want to turn around, put up roadblocks. When I feel like I can't finish, encourage me. Steady me when I stumble, carry me when I am weak. Through You I have the strength to keep walking.
Marilyn Jansen

"For I can do everything with the help of Christ who gives me the strength I need."
Philippians 4:13

God loves you, is present in you, lives in you, dwells in you, calls you, saves you, and offers you an understanding and light which are like nothing you ever found in books or heard in sermons.
Thomas Merton

Write Proverbs 3:5–6.

_____

_____

_____

_____

_____

_____

DAY SEVENTY-ONE

"For this God is our God forever and ever; He will be our guide even to the end."

Psalm 48:14 (NIV)

Cling to Christ until the life from Him—the Divine life, by that very contact, flows into your being and revives your fainting Spirit. Become recharged. Rest and regain power and strength. Then let the tide of love and joy flow in.

from *God Calling*

Thank you, dear Jesus, for the goodness and mercy you have shown me. Thank you for being my comforter and my guide. Thank you for loving me so much that you won't give up on me.

A joyful (heart) is like the sunshine of God's love, the hope of eternal happiness, the flame of burning love.

Mother Teresa

Write Psalm 9:2.

_____

_____

_____

_____

_____

_____

_____

_____

DAY SEVENTY-TWO

"These I will bring to my holy mountain and give them joy in my house of prayer; their burnt offerings and sacrifices will be accepted on my altar; for my house will be called a house of prayer."

Isaiah 56:7 (NIV)

Have you ever realized the wonder of the friendship you can have with Christ? Have you ever thought what it means to be able to summon at will the God of the world? Feel awe, feel the desire to worship Him in wondering amazement. But think, too, of the mighty tender, humble condescension of His friendship. Think of Him in the little things of everyday life.

from *God Calling*

Learn in the little daily things of life to delay action until you get *His* guidance.

from *God Calling*

Lord, make my life a little flower
That gives joy to all:
Content to bloom in nature
Although its place be small.

Mitilda Edward

"I will praise you, O Lord, with all my heart; I will tell of all your wonders. I will be glad and rejoice in you; I will sing praises to your name, O Most High."

Psalm 9:1–2 (NIV)

Give thanks to the God of the universe that He wants to call you His friend.

_____

_____

DAY SEVENTY-THREE

The mark of faith and victory is the ability to go on, and it is the finest tribute we can pay to the one whose loss we mourn. It is important to remember that sorrow and love go hand in hand, that mourning is the by-product of loving. God loves you and will bring you through the valley to the mountaintop on the other side.

James W. Moore

God is on both sides of the grave. Death is not really death at all. Rather, it is movement from one dimension of life with God to a deeper dimension of life with God. He is the Father who loves His children and who has prepared a place for us. He is the Good Shepherd, and because of Him, we can walk through the valley of the shadow of death without fear, for He is with us.

Dr. D. L. Dykes (as expressed in a funeral service)

The saving reaction is simply to go on living, to go on working, and to find in the presence of Jesus Christ the strength and courage to meet life with steady eyes.

from a William Barclay sermon

Your thoughts:

_____

_____

_____

_____

_____

_____

_____

DAY SEVENTY-FOUR

Dear Father, help me to listen to you. So often, I act like I am listening when I'm not. Help me to concentrate carefully on what your Word says. You have all the secrets for living a good life. I don't want to miss them—I want to listen.

Marilyn Jansen

Shed a little sunshine in the heart of one, that one is cheered to pass it on, and so my vitalizing joy-giving message goes. Be transmitters these days. Love and laugh. Cheer all. Love all.

from God Calling

"And now I entrust you to God and the word of His grace—His message that is able to build you up and give you an inheritance with all those He has set apart for Himself."

Acts 20:32

"And I am sure that God, who began the good work within you, will continue His work until it is finally finished on that day when Christ comes back again."

Philippians 1:6

What can you do to hear God better?

_____

_____

_____

_____

_____

_____

DAY SEVENTY-FIVE

It will be worth it all when we see Jesus. Life's trials will seem so small when we see Christ; one glimpse of His dear face all sorrow will erase, so bravely run the race till we see Christ.
Rusthoi

The gains of Heaven will more than compensate us for the losses of earth.
Dave Branon

Nothing costs as much as loving, except not loving.

"A merry heart does good, like medicine."
Proverbs 17:22a (NKJV)

Christians, above all others, should benefit from laughter because we have the greatest reason to be joyful. Our faith is firmly rooted in God, and our optimism is based on the assurance that our lives are under His wise control.
Richard DeHaan

"Friendship with the Lord is reserved for those who fear Him. With them He shares the secrets of His covenant."
Psalm 25:14

List some things you are glad about.

_____

_____

_____

_____

_____

DAY SEVENTY-SIX

"Lord, you have brought light to my life; my God, you light up my darkness."

Psalm 18:28

In prayer Jesus slows us down, teaches us to count how few days we have, and gifts us with wisdom. He reveals to us that we are so caught up in what is urgent that we have overlooked what is essential.

Brennan Manning

"Teach us to make the most of our time so that we may grow in wisdom."

Psalm 90:12

I am with you all the time controlling, blessing and helping you. No man or woman can stand against my will for you—if you trust me and place your affairs in my hands. To the passenger it may seem as if each wave would overwhelm the ship, or turn it aside from its course. The Captain knows by experience that, in spite of wind and wave, he steers a straight course to the haven where He would be. So trust me, the Captain of your salvation.

from *God Calling*

Do you have a fear that you need to replace with trust?

_____

_____

_____

_____

_____

DAY SEVENTY-SEVEN

For those who are in Jesus Christ, death is but a door from the dark tomb to a sunlit garden.

Donald G. Barnhouse

"The Lord says, 'I will guide you along the best pathway for your life. I will advise you and watch over you.'... unfailing love surrounds those who trust the Lord."

Psalm 32:8 and 10b

Being able to trust God is grounded in staking the whole of my being on the reality that He loves me.

Paula Rinehart

Many flowers open to the sun, but only one follows Him constantly. Heart, be the sunflower, not only open to receive God's blessing, but constant in looking to Him.

John Paul Richter

"But for you who fear my name, the Sun of Righteousness will rise with healing in his wings."

Malachi 4:2a

Write Psalm 39:7.

_____

_____

_____

_____

_____

_____

DAY SEVENTY-EIGHT

"[A]nd trust yourself to the God who made you, for He will never fail you ... Give all your worries and cares to God, for He cares about what happens to you."

1 Peter 4:19b and 5:7

I believe that in Heaven we will have special feelings for one another. We will love perfectly and enjoy complete healing from all the hurts of our earthly relationships. That will be more fulfilling than any marriage. The pleasures of earth cannot compare to the joys of Heaven.

Herb Vander Lugt

"For when they rise from the dead they neither marry nor are given in marriage, but are like the angels in Heaven."

Mark 12:25 (NKJV)

The love we've known while here below, in Heaven will find its highest joy; for we will know Christ's perfect love that memories cannot destroy.

D. DeHaan

You are mine. Once I have set on you My stamp and seal of ownership, all my hosts throng to serve and protect you. Remember that you are a child of the King.

from *God Calling*

Your thoughts:

_____

_____

_____

_____

_____

DAY SEVENTY-NINE

Prayer is more than an option—it should be a life style. When you talk to God daily, his peace will envelop your heart. Don't miss out on your audience with the King!

Its supports may be out of your sight, hidden in the secret place of the Most High, but if I have asked you to step on and up firmly, then surely have I secured your ladder ... I complete every task committed to me. So trust and be not afraid.

from God Calling

Know my divine power. Trust in Me. Dwell in my love. Laugh and trust. Laughter is a child's faith in God and good.

from God Calling

Find that He is the greatest treasure of our lives. *Discover* that knowing Him is the source of genuine satisfaction.

David McCasland

"Pray without ceasing."

1 Thessalonians 5:17 (KJV)

Write a prayer that you could pray morning, noon, and night.

_____

_____

_____

_____

_____

_____

_____

DAY EIGHTY

"For everyone who asks, receives. Everyone who seeks, finds. And the door is opened to everyone who knocks."
Matthew 7:8

Our actions and reactions show whether we really know the Lord Jesus.
Joanie Yoder

What a mighty thing it is to live for God's Kingdom! Live for it; look for it—it is so powerful it will completely overwhelm you.
J. Heinrich Arnold

A Christian should be continually composing new songs of praise around the fresh mercies of God.
Mart DeHaan

"My only hope is in your unfailing love and faithfulness."
Psalm 40:11b

Jesus *is* the answer!

Lift your eyes heavenward and think of your loved one enjoying God's presence. Describe what you see in your mind.

_____

_____

_____

_____

_____

_____

DAY EIGHTY-ONE

It was on the quiet mountain slopes that I taught my disciples the truths of my Kingdom, not during the storm. You are passing through a storm. Enough that I am with you to say, "Peace be still," to quiet both wind and waves.

from *God Calling*

Be joyful in knowing that Jesus is not only your guide, but your friend as well!

"Blessed be God, who didn't turn away when I was praying and didn't refuse me His kindness and love."

Psalm 66:20 (TLB)

"Give thanks to the Lord, for He is good; His faithful love endures forever."

1 Chronicles 16:34

"Praise the Lord; Praise God my Savior! For each day He carries me in His arms."

Psalm 68:19

Prayer unites the soul to God.

Julian of Norwich

Give praise to God for loving you.

_____

_____

_____

_____

_____

DAY EIGHTY-TWO

"I am the vine, you are the branches. When you are joined with me and I with you, the relation intimate and organic, the harvest is sure to be abundant."

John 15:5 (*The Message*)

Carry out my commands and leave the result to Me. Remember that the commands I have given you have been already worked out by Me in the spirit world to produce, in your case and in your circumstances, the required result. So follow my rules faithfully.

from *God Calling*

Make the Bible your delight. God will give you passion for His eternal word if you are a truth seeker.

Dave Branon

"How sweet are your words to my taste; they are sweeter than honey. Your word is a lamp for my feet and a light for my path."

Psalm 119:103 & 105

Write Psalm 92:4.

_____

_____

_____

_____

_____

_____

_____

_____

DAY EIGHTY-THREE

When trouble comes, think of all you have to be thankful for. Praise, praise, praise! Say thank-you all the time. This is the remover of mountains—your thankful heart of praise.

from *God Calling*

"We wait in hope for the Lord; He is our help and our shield. In Him our hearts rejoice, for we trust in His Holy name. May your unfailing love rest upon us, O Lord, even as we put our hope in You."

Psalm 33:20–22 (NIV)

A wonderful future is before you; a future of unlimited power to bless others. Just be a channel.

from *God Calling*

Dear Jesus, take my heart and hand and grant me this, I pray: that I through your sweet love may grow more like you day by day.

Garrison

Living daily for Christ requires dying daily to self.

David Roper

That is a description of my loved one's life—living for others.

Your thoughts:

_____

_____

_____

_____

_____

_____

DAY EIGHTY-FOUR

"But as for me, I trust in You, O Lord; I say, 'You are my God.' My times are in Your hand."
Psalm 31:14–15a (NKJV)

When I found truth, there I found my God who *is* the truth. And there since the time I learned You, You live in my memory; and there I find You, whenever I call You to remembrance, and delight in You.
Augustine

"For the Lord is good; His mercy is everlasting and His truth endures to all generations."
Psalm 100:5 (NKJV)

"Return to the Lord . . . and my love will know no bounds . . . I am the one who looks after you and cares for you."
Hosea 14:1a, 4b, 8b

Obey Jesus. His love for you is indescribably great!

Make of list of those you love.

_____

_____

_____

_____

_____

_____

_____

_____

_____

DAY EIGHTY-FIVE

Keep close to Me and you shall know the way because as I said to my disciples, I am the way. That is the solution to all earth's problems. Keep close, very close to Me. Think, act and live in my presence. That is the secret of all power, all peace, all purity, all influence—the keeping very near to Me.

from God Calling

Every breath we draw is a gift of His love, every moment of existence a gift of grace.

Thomas Merton

"The Lord longs to be gracious to you; He rises to show you compassion. For the Lord is a God of justice. Blessed are all who wait for Him!"

Isaiah 30:18 (NIV)

Happiness isn't found by pursuing it. It is a by-product of seeking an ever closer walk with God.

Herb Vander Lugt

"Taste and see that the Lord is good; oh the joys of those who trust in Him!"

Psalm 34:8

How has the grieving process drawn you to a closer walk with God?

_____

_____

_____

_____

_____

_____

DAY EIGHTY-SIX

Death is temporary—-life is eternal.

Father forgive me for feeding the cravings of my sinful flesh. Help me to cultivate instead the tastes that your Holy Spirit wants to produce in me. Help me to learn to savor the flavor of Godliness.
Mart DeHaan

"For we are the temple of the living God. As God said: 'I will live in them and walk among them . . . And I will be your Father and you will be my sons and daughters,' says the Lord Almighty."
2 Corinthians 6:16b and 18

What a wonderful privilege!

His strength is not for my success or well-being, but so that I will glorify Christ by living in His power.
David McCasland

People are like stained glass windows: they sparkle and shine when the sun is out, but when the darkness sets in, their true beauty is revealed only if there is light within.
Elizabeth Kubler-Ross

Your thoughts:

_____

_____

_____

_____

_____

_____

DAY EIGHTY-SEVEN

Heaven is to the dying Christian, as the fireside of home is to the weary traveler who has forced his way over bleak moor and through blinding storm.

Unknown source

"The righteous pass away; the godly often die before their time … no one seems to understand that God is protecting them from the evil to come. For the godly who die will rest in peace."

Isaiah 57:1–2

"The Lord will guide you always; He will satisfy your needs in a sun-scorched land … you will be like a well-watered garden, like a spring whose waters never fail."

Isaiah 58:11 (NIV)

"The high and lofty one who inhabits eternity, the Holy One, says this: 'I live in that high and holy place with those whose spirits are contrite and humble. I refresh the humble and give new courage to those with repentant hearts.'"

Isaiah 57:15

God is *so* great! And my loved one is already with Him in that "High and Holy place."

Lord, I thank you for the promise of the resurrection.

_____

_____

_____

_____

_____

DAY EIGHTY-EIGHT

There is no bond of union on earth to compare with the union between a soul that loves Christ—and Christ. Priceless beyond all earth's imaginings is that friendship.

from *God Calling*

Each of us can participate in celebrating God's majesty by glorifying Him with our lives.

Dave Branon

"Give thanks to the Lord for He is good! His faithful love endures forever."

Psalm 118:29

The human spirit can gain new hope from an encouraging word.

Joanie Yoder

Prayer opens the way for God to work.

Bible study notes on 1 Samuel 1:10

In prayer, God hears more than words; He listens to your heart.

David McCasland

Write a heartfelt prayer to the Lord.

_____

_____

_____

_____

_____

DAY EIGHTY-NINE

His grace can cause His beauty to be seen in you.
Dave Branon

If you could know my love, if you could measure my longing to help, you would know that I need no agonizing pleading. Your *need* is my call.
from *God Calling*

It is the heart that prays. It is to the voice of the heart that God listens, and it is the heart that He answers.
Jean-Nicholas Grou

"Then you will call upon me and come and pray to me, and I will listen to you. You will seek me and find me when you seek me with all your heart."
Jeremiah 29:12–13 (NIV)

The love of God is my pillow, soft and healing and wide;
I rest my soul in its comfort, and in its calm I abide.
Long

Only God can fill the emptiness of an aching heart.
Mart DeHaan

Ask God to fill the void in your heart.

_____

_____

_____

_____

_____

_____

DAY NINETY

It is right and good that we, for all things, and in all places, and at all times, give thanks and praise to you, O God. We worship you, we confess to you, we praise you, we bless you, we sing to you, and we give thanks to you: Maker, Nourisher, Guardian, Healer, Lord and Father of all.
Lancelot Andrewes

"Praise and glory and wisdom and thanks and honor and power and strength be to our God for ever and ever. Amen!"
Revelation 7:12 (NIV)

My keeping power is never at fault, but only your realization of it. Not whether I *can* provide a shelter from the storm, but your failure to be sure of the security of that shelter.
from *God Calling*

Rely on Christ alone. To hold back, to retain, implies a fear of the future, a want of trust in Him. Trust wholly. Trust completely. Empty your vessel. He will fill it. Depend on Him.
from *God Calling*

In what areas of your life do you need to trust Him more?

_____

_____

_____

_____

_____

_____

_____

DAY NINETY-ONE

Use now what God has given you, count not its worth as small;
God does not ask of you great things, just faithfulness—that's all.
Bosch

Remember a happy, peaceful time in your past. Rest there. Each moment has a richness that takes a lifetime to savor.
Grandstaff

"I am with you and will watch over you wherever you go ... I will not leave you until I have done what I have promised you."
Genesis 28:15 (NIV)

"I call on you, O God, for you will answer me; give ear to me and hear my prayer. Show the wonder of your great love . . . Keep me as the apple of your eye; hide me in the shadow of your wings."
Psalm 17:6-7a & 8 (NIV)

Jesus, thou art watching over me to bless and care for me. Yes! Remember that always—that out of darkness I am leading you to light. Out of unrest, to rest, out of disorder, to order. Out of faults and failure to perfection. So trust me wholly. Fear nothing. Hope ever. Look ever up to Me and I will be your sure aid.
from *God Calling*

Your thoughts:

_____

_____

_____

_____

_____

DAY NINETY-TWO

Amazing Savior

Amazing is the love my Savior
Demonstrates to me;
Persevering humbly
As He hung upon that tree.

Imagine that the Son of God
Would carry me each day,
Guiding and instructing me;
Hearing when I pray.

Wonderful His majesty;
I am in awe of Him!
He is the great Redeemer,
Whose light will never dim.

Holy is my Father;
Yet He wants to be my friend.
I am a grateful daughter
And will serve Him till the end.

Luan Louis

Your thoughts:

_____

_____

_____

_____

_____

DAY NINETY-THREE

"May the Lord make your love increase and overflow for each other and for everyone else, just as ours does for you."
1 Thessalonians 3:12 (NIV)

Love overrides every objection. No logical argument can overthrow it. The goodness of God revealed in our love draws people to repentance.
David Roper

We need to break out our best perfumes for the living. Give praise to others while they are here; they won't need it in the hereafter.
Haddon Robinson

When people look at us, they need to see what God has accomplished in our lives.
Bible study notes on Genesis 14:20

When Jesus purchased us with His blood on the cross, He didn't get only a portion of us. He owns everything. So why do we sometimes live as if parts of us don't belong to Jesus? That's not fair to the buyer. Christ bought us—body, soul and spirit. Let's make sure we let Him use the total package for His glory.
Dave Branon

How can you show God's love to someone today?

_____

_____

_____

_____

_____

_____

DAY NINETY-FOUR

"He never grows faint or weary. No one can measure the depths of His understanding. He gives power to those who are tired and worn out; He offers strength to the weak."
Isaiah 40:28b–29

Don't limit His work in your life by underestimating Him. God's power and strength never diminish.
Bible study notes from Isaiah 40: 28–29

Sunshine helps to make glad the heart of man. It is the laughter of nature. Nature is often God's nurse for tired souls and weary bodies.
from *God Calling*

Small deeds done are better than great deeds planned. We know that we cannot do everything, but help us to do something, for Jesus' sake.
Peter Marshall

Who do you know that could use your help today? Write a prayer for them.

_____

_____

_____

_____

_____

_____

_____

_____

_____

_____

DAY NINETY-FIVE

Tune in to the music of Heaven and sing a new song with the angels.
David Roper

It is not in the way, but the loving rejoicing in the way and the guidance that matters with my disciples. Rejoice in the little daily stones of the way. Across the grayest days there are the gleams of "Sonlight".
from *God Calling*

Kneeling in a spirit of humility, turn your eyes Heavenward and realize the majesty, the power, the beauty that may be yours. Remember there are no limits to My giving—there may be to your accepting. Oh rejoice at the wonders to which you are called, and seeing them in prayer, rise in My strength, filled with the longing to attain them.
from *God Calling*

Give yourself and all you have ever met a fresh start from today. Remember no more your sins and failures. The remembrance is a current of disappointment that hinders the swimmer.
from *God Calling*

Ask God to help you keep your focus on Him.

_____

_____

_____

_____

_____

_____

_____

DAY NINETY-SIX

Clipped wings can grow again. Broken voices regain a strength and beauty unknown before. Your power to help other lives will soon bring its delight, even when at first, the help to yourself may seem too late to bring you joy. "Behold, I make all things new."

from *God Calling*

If you walk with God and have a consistent prayer life, then sensitivity develops between you and your heavenly Father.

Luis Palau

"He rescued me because He delights in me."

Psalm 18:19

"Yet I am not alone because the Father is with me."

John 16:32b

Those who know Jesus are never alone.

Write Joshua 1:9.

_____

_____

_____

_____

_____

_____

_____

_____

DAY NINETY-SEVEN

All things are possible with my Master, my Lord, my Friend. This truth accepted and firmly believed in is the ladder up which a soul can climb from the lowest of pits to the sublimest of heights.

from *God Calling*

"For I can do everything with the help of Christ who gives me the strength I need."

Philippians 4:13

Though my way may seem a narrow way, it yet leads to life, abundant life. Follow it. It is not so narrow but that I can tread it beside you.

from *God Calling*

And if He could raise Lazarus from the dead after he was in the tomb for four days, is there anything He cannot do for you or me? What miracle do you think is beyond His power to accomplish? When you don't understand why, just trust Him! Understand that *you may not understand* this side of Heaven. Respect God's silences. Claim through your own experience, the blessing that follows brokenness, the life that follows death, and the glory that follows suffering. Trust Him! He will bring you through.

Anne Graham Lotz

Your thoughts:

_____

_____

_____

_____

_____

_____

DAY NINETY-EIGHT

From now a new life is opening out before you. Yours to enter into the Kingdom I have prepared for you. The sunlight of my presence is on your path. Trust and go forward unafraid. My grace is sufficient for all your needs.

from *God Calling*

"In quietness and confidence is your strength."
Isaiah 30:15b

Allow God to act.

"Don't worry about anything; instead, pray about everything. Tell God what you need and thank Him for all he has done. If you do this, you will experience God's peace which is far more wonderful than the human mind can understand. His peace will guard your hearts and minds as you live in Christ Jesus."
Philippians 4:6–7

As you pray, invite God to work His will through your life. Prayer has power to change *us* as well as our circumstances.

Write Romans 15:13.

_____

_____

_____

_____

_____

_____

DAY NINETY-NINE

God may break up our comfortable nests now and then, but behind every difficult change lays His love and eternal purpose. He is not cruel or capricious; He is working for our ultimate good. He wants us to be "conformed to the image of His Son" (Romans 8:29 KJV) and to give us glorious enjoyment in Heaven forever. How then can we fear change when it comes from someone whose love for us never changes?
David Roper

"I will bless You every day and I will praise You forever and ever … I will meditate on your majestic, glorious splendor and your wonderful miracles."
Psalm 145:2a, 5

The sudden precious moments in life need to be recognized for the unique periods they are, not wasted by wishing for something else.
Edith Schaeffer

God invites us to actively pursue the opportunities at hand instead of lamenting over what we don't have.
David McCasland

Read Philippians 3:13–14 and write how it can apply to you.

_____

_____

_____

_____

_____

_____

DAY ONE HUNDRED

Every loss leaves an empty space that only God's presence can fill.
Anne Cetas

"Through each day the Lord pours His unfailing love upon me . . . I will put my hope in God! I will praise Him again—my Savior and my God!"
Psalm 42:8a, 11b

Lift up your head from earth's troubles and view the glories of the Kingdom. Higher and higher each day see more of Heaven. Speak to Me. Long for Me. Rest in Me. Abide in Me.
from *God Calling*

Thank you for the love of friends,
For joy ahead when this life ends,
For childlike faith that's unrestrained,
And saving grace my soul has gained.

"The joy of the Lord is my strength."
Nehemiah 8:10c

Write Psalm 139:9–10.

_____

_____

_____

_____

_____

_____

_____

_____

DAY ONE HUNDRED ONE

The face is a mirror of the heart—let people see Jesus in yours.

"We can be mirrors that brightly reflect the glory of the Lord. And as the spirit of the Lord works within us, we become more and more like Him and reflect His glory even more."
2 Corinthians 3:18b

A consciousness of My presence as love makes all life different. Beyond all words is My love and care for you. Walk in My love.
from *God Calling*

"The eternal God is your refuge, and His everlasting arms are under you."
Deuteronomy 33:27

In life, we often have to walk down unfamiliar paths. So how do we do that without making costly mistakes? We take *Someone* along who knows the way. "Lead me, O Lord, in Your righteousness … make Your way straight before my face." (Psalm 5:8 KJV)
Dave Branon

Death is not extinguishing the light; it is putting out the lamp because the dawn has come.
Rabindranath Tagore

Your thoughts:

_____

_____

_____

_____

DAY ONE HUNDRED TWO

Have no fear for the future. Be quiet, be still, and in that very stillness your strength will come and will be maintained.

from *God Calling*

Let there be no hurry in your plans. You live not in time but in eternity. It is in the unseen that your life-future is being planned.

from *God Calling*

Put all fear of the future aside. *Know* that you will be led. *Know* that you will be shown. I have promised.

from *God Calling*

"His compassions never fail. They are new every morning; great is your faithfulness ... The Lord is good to those whose hope is in Him, to the one who seeks Him."

Lamentations 3:22–23, 25 (NIV)

"The Lord will work out His plans for my life—for your faithful love, O Lord, endures forever. Don't abandon me, for you made me ... You chart the path ahead of me and tell me where to stop and rest. Every moment you know where I am."

Psalm 138:8 and 139:3

Thank God for His great wisdom and compassion.

_____

_____

_____

_____

_____

_____

DAY ONE HUNDRED THREE

Out of all possible paths, He has chosen the best, the route most adapted to who we are and what He has in store for us.

David Roper

Search for the joy in life. Hunt for it as for hidden treasure. Love and laugh. *Delight* yourself in the Lord.

from *God Calling*

Just leave in His hands the present and the future, knowing only that God is good.

from *God Calling*

"Trust in the Lord with all thine heart and lean not to thine own understanding. In all thy ways acknowledge Him and He will direct thy path."

Proverbs 3:5–6 (KJV)

List a goal you can strive for.

_____

_____

_____

_____

_____

_____

_____

_____

_____

DAY ONE HUNDRED FOUR

All the love and the strength and beauty you have seen in Me are in My Father. If you see that, and know Him and Me as we really are, then that is really sufficient for you—completes your life—satisfies you—is all you need.

from *God Calling*

"Show me where to walk, for I have come to you in prayer . . . Teach me to do your will, for you are my God. May your gracious Spirit lead me forward on firm footing."

Psalm 143:8b, 10a

Life-changing events do not happen by accident. They are not determined by the stars. They are not by chance. There is no such thing as chance. The Lord uses every situation in life to accomplish His purposes. We should begin each day with a sincere desire to please the Lord, gladly anticipating His appointments for us.

Richard DeHaan

How can you encourage someone else today?

_____

_____

_____

_____

_____

_____

_____

_____

DAY ONE HUNDRED FIVE

We still grieve when a believing loved one dies. Grief is love's expression. But beneath it all is an unshakable joy because we know our loved one is in Heaven.
Dave Egner

Take all that happens as My planning. All is well. I have all prepared in My love. Let your heart sing.
from God Calling

Your insights need to grow as your relationship with Christ deepens, as you open chambers of your heart to the Holy Spirit's control. He is your truly special resource. The Spirit alone provides the Master's touch.
Les Stobbe

When you look to Me for guidance, My hand is laid upon your arm, a gentle touch to point the way.
from God Calling

Lord, give me counsel in my anxiety, help in time of trial, comfort when persecuted, and strength against every temptation.
Latin, eleventh century

Your thoughts:

_____

_____

_____

_____

_____

_____

DAY ONE HUNDRED SIX

"I will instruct you and teach you in the way you should go; I will counsel you and watch over you."
Psalm 32:8 (NIV)

Let me forget the hurt and pain found along life's way;
Let me remember kindnesses given day by day.
Berry

In my universe, for every task I give one of my children, there is set aside all that is necessary for its performance. So why fear? So why doubt? Face each difficulty sure that the wisdom and strength will be given you for it. Claim it.
from *God Calling*

Rejoice! These are your wilderness days. But surely and safely, you are being led to your Canaan of plenty.
from *God Calling*

Write Jeremiah 29:11.

_____

_____

_____

_____

_____

_____

_____

_____

_____

DAY ONE HUNDRED SEVEN

Oh! My children, draw very near to Me. See Me as I really am, that you may have the joy of finding in Me all you could desire. The fulfillment of all you could desire in Master, Lord or Friend.

from *God Calling*

Help me remember that your Word tells me that rain falls on the righteous and the unrighteous—that I should praise You for who You are, not for how much You give me. Help me to remember that the part of the picture I see is very small and that You see the whole thing. Help me trust You.

Could I fail you? Just know it is not possible.

from *God Calling*

Yes, I know all; every cry for mercy; every sigh of weariness; every plea for help; every sorrow over failure; every weakness. I am with you through all. I am beside you. Lean on My love.

from *God Calling*

Write Matthew 28:20b.

_____

_____

_____

_____

_____

_____

_____

DAY ONE HUNDRED EIGHT

Remember, God knows what we need, and our deepest needs are spiritual. David was saying that if you have God, you have all you really need. God is enough. God may allow you to go without to help you grow more dependent on Him. He may want you to learn that you need Him more than you need your immediate desires met.

Bible study notes on Psalm 34:9–10

When Jesus comes, it will be in the greatest processional of all. And He will take us away, far above this world. Our finite minds cannot fathom the place He is preparing. But we do know we will live forever without shedding a tear; we do know we will have eternal peace, and best of all, we do know we will be with Jesus face to face. We will be reunited with loved ones. There will be harmony, security, and the sweet comfort of family and friends.

Dee Brestin and Kathy Trocolli

List those you look forward to seeing again in Heaven.

_____

_____

_____

_____

_____

_____

_____

_____

_____

_____

DAY ONE HUNDRED NINE

As all reform is from within out, you will always find the outward has improved, too. To do this is to release the imprisoned God-Power within you. That power, once operative, will immediately perform miracles (in you). Then indeed shall your mourning be turned into joy.

from *God Calling*

"The Lord is my strength and my song; He has become my victory."

Exodus 15:2

In I Kings 19:5–18 the Lord knew Elijah needed restoration, so He provided for His needs. He revealed Himself to him and renewed Elijah's sense of purpose by giving him work to do. God brought him hope by reminding him that he was not alone. Look to God; He is your source of hope.

Anne Cetas

These things are all true for me, too. God knew I needed restoration. He has provided so well for me. He has revealed Himself to me through His Spirit and renewed my sense of purpose by giving me work to do.

I am not alone. God is with me, and He is my source of hope.

Your thoughts:

_____

_____

_____

_____

_____

_____

_____

LOVE IS ETERNAL

Love goes on forever
When two souls are joined as one.
One's heart just keeps on beating
While the other one is gone.

He was the one I turned to
For all things until the end.
My strength, my joy, my confidant;
He was my greatest friend.

My sadness turns to joy
As I reflect upon my loss;
My strong and earthly warrior
Was a soldier of the cross.

I know love is eternal
And when my days on earth are through,
He'll reach for me and say,
"I have been waiting here for you."

Luan Louis

Dedicated to Jeff Henschen

STAR LIGHT

High above the stars so bright
My love is shining in the light
Of his creator, God, and King
And with the angels he does sing.

Hallelujah, glory, praises,
Grateful thanks in my heart raises,
Knowing that our loved ones thrive
Because of Christ who is alive!

All the saints who've gone before us
Join together in a chorus,
Waiting for that glorious day
When we arrive, with them to stay.

So as the stars shine in the sky
Reminding me of days gone by,
Let my life be a shining ray
Helping others find the way.

Luan Louis

INVITATION

Perhaps you have read this journal and wish you could have the assurance of hope for eternity, but have never asked Jesus into your heart. If you are feeling the Spirit's call to do so, I encourage you to take that step. You simply ask Him to forgive you of your sins and tell Him you believe that He died for all of us and rose again. You trust Him as your Redeemer and believe that He is the only way of salvation. You believe that He is living in Heaven and because you trust Him as your Savior, you will join Him there one day.

"For all have sinned, all fall short of God's glorious standard. Yet now God in His gracious kindness declares us not guilty. He has done this through Christ Jesus, who has freed us by taking away our sins. For God sent Jesus to take the punishment for our sins and to satisfy God's anger against us. We are made right with God when we believe that Jesus shed His blood, sacrificing His life for us."
Romans 3:23–25a

"Christ died and rose again for this very purpose, so that he might be Lord of those who are alive and of those who have died."
Romans 14:9

"For God so loved the world that He gave His only son, so that everyone who believes in Him will not perish, but have eternal life."
John 3:16

"Jesus told Him, 'I am the way, the truth, and the life. No one can come to the Father except through me.'"
John 14:6

"I assure you, those who listen to my message and believe in God who sent me have eternal life. They will never be condemned for their sins, but they have already passed from death into life."
John 5:24

If you have taken this step today, welcome to the family of God!

"There is joy in the presence of God's angels when even one sinner repents."

Luke 15:10

I urge you to follow up this decision by seeking a local fundamental church where you can fellowship and worship with other believers and grow in your faith.

Write your own prayer in the space below.

_____

_____

_____

_____

_____

_____

_____

_____

_____

_____

_____

_____

_____

_____

_____

_____

APPENDIX

Scriptures Listed in the Daily Prompts

DAY TEN
Psalm 100: "Shout with joy to the Lord, O earth! Worship the Lord with gladness. Come before him, singing with joy. Acknowledge that the Lord is God! He made us, and we are his. We are his people, the sheep of his pasture. Enter his gates with thanksgiving; go into his courts with praise. Give thanks to him and bless his name. For the Lord is good. His unfailing love continues forever, and his faithfulness continues to each generation."

DAY ELEVEN
Psalm 121:5: "The Lord Himself watches over you! The Lord stands beside you as your protective shade."

DAY FIFTY
Hebrews 10:23: "Without wavering, let us hold tightly to the hope we say we have, for God can be trusted to keep his promise."

DAY SIXTY-TWO
Psalm 34:7: "For the angel of the Lord guards all who fear him, [through good and bad], and he rescues them."

DAY SIXTY-EIGHT
Psalm 42:11: "Why am I discouraged? Why so sad? I will put my hope in God! I will praise Him again—my savior and my God."

DAY SEVENTY
Proverbs 3:5–6: "Trust in the Lord with all your heart; do not depend on your own understanding. Seek his will in all you do, and he will direct your paths."

DAY SEVENTY-ONE
Psalm 9:2: "I will be filled with joy because of you. I will sing praises to your name, O Most High."

DAY SEVENTY-SEVEN
Psalm 39:7 "And so, Lord, where do I put my hope? My only hope is in you."

DAY EIGHTY-TWO
Psalm 92:4: "You thrill me, Lord, with all you have done for me! I sing for joy because of what you have done."

DAY NINETY-SIX
Joshua 1:9: "I command you—be strong and courageous! Do not be afraid or discouraged. For the Lord your God is with you wherever you go."

DAY NINETY-EIGHT
Romans 15:13: "So I pray that God, who gives you hope, will keep you happy and full of peace as you believe in him. May you overflow with hope through the power of the Holy Spirit."

DAY NINETY-NINE
Philippians 3:13–14: "No, dear brothers and sisters, I am still not all I should be, but I am focusing all my energies on this one thing: Forgetting the past and looking forward to what lies ahead, I strain to reach the end of the race and receive the prize for which God, through Christ Jesus is calling us up to Heaven."

DAY ONE HUNDRED
Psalm 139:9–10: "If I ride the wings of the morning, if I dwell by the farthest oceans, even there your hand will guide me, and your strength will support me."

DAY ONE HUNDRED SIX
Jeremiah 29:11: "For I know the plans I have for you, says the Lord. They are plans for good and not for disaster, to give you a future and a hope."

DAY ONE HUNDRED SEVEN
Matthew 28:20b: "And be sure of this: I am with you always, even to the end of the age."

BIBLIOGRAPHY

The 2004 *Sharing Our Faith* devotional was published by Faith Alliance Church, New Bremen, OH. Special thanks goes to the following contributors to that devotional: Shirley James, Patty Schultze, Dean Greenwood, Ted Wagner, and Carmen Hirschfeld.

Quotes from authors Paula Rinehart and Marilyn Jansen were used with their permission.

The poem by Lisa O. Engelhardt was used with her permission.

DAY TWO

The Great Themes of Scripture: Old Testament, © 1988, by Richard Rohr and Joseph Martos. Reprinted with permission of St. Anthony Messenger Press, 28 W. Liberty St., Cincinnati, OH 45202. www.sampbooks.org.

DAY THREE

Scripture taken from *The Message.* © 1993, 1994, 1995, 1996, 2000, 2001, 2002. Used by permission of NavPress Publishing Group, Colorado Springs, CO 80935

DAY FOUR

Cicero 106BC-43BC was a Roman statesman, philosopher and author. His works are in the public domain.

Henry Ward Beecher 1813-1887 was a Congregationalist Minister. His works are in the public domain.

DAY TWELVE

© 2010 DAYSpring Cards. Used by permission, all rights reserved. www.DAYspring.com.

DAY FOURTEEN

Emily Matthews poem reproduced by permission from American Greetings Corporation,Cleveland, OH. © AGC, LLC

DAY EIGHTEEN

Martin Luther 1483-1546 was a German priest and professor. His works are in the public domain.

Joanie Yoder, *Our Daily Bread,* © 2004 by RBC Ministries, Grand Rapids, MI. Reprinted by permission. All rights reserved.

DAY NINETEEN

The words by Mark Henschen were written as a tribute to his brother, Jeff.

DAY TWENTY

© DAYSpring Cards. Used by permission, all rights reserved. www. DAYspring.com.

Poem by Bee Ewing was from a framed gift I received. I thank her for her ministry to those who are grieving.

DAY TWENTY-TWO

One Minute After You Die by Erwin Lutzer, 1997. Moody Publishers, 820 N. LaSalle Blvd., Chicago, IL

Quote by Jim Elliot used by permission of Lars Gren.

DAY TWENTY-THREE

© 2010 DAYSpring Cards. Used by permission, all rights reserved. www. DAYspring.com.

DAY TWENTY-FOUR

Morris and Dave Branon, *Our Daily Bread,* © 2004 by RBC Ministries, Grand Rapids, MI. Reprinted by permission. All rights reserved.

DAY TWENTY-FIVE

When Life Gets Tough by Henry Gariepy, 2003, Honor Books, Colorado Springs, CO

DAY TWENTY-EIGHT

David Roper, *Our Daily Bread,* © 2004 by RBC Ministries, Grand Rapids, MI. Reprinted by permission. All rights reserved.

DAY THIRTY-ONE

Dave Branon, *Our Daily Bread,* © 2004 by RBC Ministries, Grand Rapids, MI. Reprinted by permission. All rights reserved.

DAY THIRTY-FOUR

John Newton 1725-1807 was a clergyman and former ship captain. He wrote the hymn, "Amazing Grace." This excerpt is from that hymn. His works are in the public domain.

David McCasland, *Our Daily Bread,* © 2004 by RBC Ministries, Grand Rapids, MI. Reprinted by permission.

DAY THIRTY-FIVE

Mart DeHaan, *Our Daily Bread,* © 2004 by RBC Ministries, Grand Rapids, MI. Reprinted by permission.

DAY THIRY-SIX

Francis of Assisi 1181-1226 was a catholic priest and preacher. His works are in the public domain.

DAY THIRTY-SEVEN

David McCasland, *Our Daily Bread,* © 2004 by RBC Ministries, Grand Rapids, MI. Reprinted by permission.

DAY THIRTY-NINE

A Prayer For Light by Fr. Wally Hyclak, St. Marys of the Falls Catholic Church, Olmstead, OH. Used by permission

DAY FORTY-ONE

Dave Branon and D. DeHaan; *Our Daily Bread,* © 2004 by RBC Ministries, Grand Rapids, MI. Reprinted by permission.

DAY FORTY-THREE

David Roper, *Our Daily Bread,* © 2004 by RBC Ministries, Grand Rapids, MI. Reprinted by permission.

Henry Van Dyke 1852-1933 was an author, educator and clergyman. His works are in the public domain.

DAYS FORTY-FOUR and FORTY-FIVE

Taken from *The Purpose Driven Life* by Rick Warren. © 2002 by Rick Warren. Used by permission of Zondervan, www.zondervan.com.

DAY FORTY-SIX

From *And the Angels Were Silent* by Max Lucado, © 1987, Thomas Nelson Inc., Nashville, TN. Reprinted by permission. All rights reserved.

DAY FORTY-SEVEN

Julie Ackerman Link, Sper, and David McCasland, *Our Daily Bread,* © 2004 by RBC Ministries, Grand Rapids, MI. Reprinted by permission.

DAY FORTY-NINE

Grace for the Moment by Max Lucado, © 2000, Thomas Nelson Inc., Nashville, TN. Reprinted by permission. All rights reserved.

© DAYSpring Cards. Used by permission, all rights reserved. www. DAYspring.com.

DAY FIFTY-ONE

Joanie Yoder, *Our Daily Bread,* © 2004 by RBC Ministries, Grand Rapids, MI. Reprinted by permission.

DAY FIFTY-TWO

Berg and Dave Branon, *Our Daily Bread,* © 2004 by RBC Ministries, Grand Rapids, MI. Reprinted by permission.

DAY FIFTY-THREE

Quote by Elisabeth Elliot used by permission of Lars Gren.

John Newton 1725-1807 His works are in the public domain.

DAY FIFTY-FOUR

David McCasland, Sper, and Herb Vander Lugt, *Our Daily Bread,* © 2004, by RBC Ministries, Grand Rapids, MI. Used by permission.

Quote by Dale Evans Rogers can be found on QuotesDaddy.com

DAY FIFTY-FIVE

Mart and K. DeHaan, *Our Daily Bread,* © 2004 by RBC Ministries, Grand Rapids, MI. Used by permission.

DAY SEVENTY

Anne Bradstreet 1612-1672 was a 17th century poet. Her works are in the public domain.

Thoughts in Solitude by Thomas Merton, published by Farrar, Straus, Giroux. Used by permission.

DAY SEVENTY-ONE

Quote by Mother Teresa used by permission of The Mother Teresa Center, Sr. M. Annaleah, MC.

DAY SEVENTY-TWO

From *Hymn For a Little Child* by Matilda Edwards 1836-1919. This is in the public domain

DAY SEVENTY-THREE

When Grief Breaks Your Heart by James W. Moore, © 1995 by Abingdon Press, Nashville, TN Used by permission. Included in this book is the excerpt from the funeral service of his mother, performed by Dr.D.L.Dykes. Also included is the sermon excerpt by William Barclay.

DAY SEVENTY-FIVE

Rusthoi, Dave Branon and Richard DeHaan, *Our Daily Bread,* © 2004 by RBC Ministries, Grand Rapids, MI. Reprinted by permission. All rights reserved.

DAY SEVENTY-SIX

Quote by Brennan Manning used by permission of Willie Juan Ministries.

DAY SEVENTY-SEVEN

John Paul Richter, *New Dictionary of Thoughts, A Cyclopedia of Quotations* compiled by Tryon Edwards, published by Standard Book Co. New York, NY.

Quote by Donald Barnhouse used by permission of the Institute for the Study of American Evangelicals, Wheaton College, Wheaton, IL

DAY SEVENTY-EIGHT

Herb Vander Lugt and D. DeHaan, *Our Daily Bread,* © by RBC Ministries, Grand Rapids, MI. Reprinted by permission. All rights reserved.

DAY SEVENTY-NINE

David McCasland, *Our Daily Bread,* © by RBC Ministries, Grand Rapids, MI. Reprinted by permission. All rights reserved.

DAY EIGHTY

Joanie Yoder and Mart DeHaan, *Our Daily Bread,* © by RBC Ministries, Grand Rapids, MI. Reprinted by permission. All rights reserved.

Quote by J. Heinrich Arnold used by permission of Plough Publishing, publishing house of Church Communities International.

DAY EIGHTY-ONE

Julian of Norwich 1342-1416 was a medieval religious writer. Her works are in the public domain

DAY EIGHTY-TWO

Scripture taken from *The Message.* © 1993, 1994, 1995, 1996, 2000, 2001, 2002. Used by permission of NavPress Publishing Group, Colorado Springs, CO

Dave Branon, *Our Daily Bread,* © by RBC Ministries, Grand Rapids, MI. Reprinted by permission. All rights reserved.

DAY EIGHTY-THREE

Garrison and David Roper, *Our Daily Bread,* © by RBC Ministries, Grand Rapids, MI. Reprinted by permission. All rights reserved.

DAY EIGHTY-FOUR

St. Augustine of Hippo 354-430 was a philosopher and theologian. His works are in the public domain.

DAY EIGHTY-FIVE

Quote by Thomas Merton taken from *Thoughts in Solitude*, published by Farrar, Straus, Giroux. Used by permission.

Herbert Vander Lugt, *Our Daily Bread,* © 2004 by RBC Ministries, Grand Rapids, MI. Reprinted by permission. All rights reserved.

DAY EIGHTY-SIX

Mart DeHaan and David McCasland, *Our Daily Bread,* © 2004 by RBC Ministries. Reprinted by permission. All rights reserved.

Quote by Elizabeth Kubler-Ross used by permission from Ken Ross, EKR Foundation.

DAY EIGHTY-EIGHT

Dave Branon, Joanie Yoder, and David McCasland, *Our Daily Bread,* © 2004 by RBC Ministries. Reprinted by permission. All rights reserved.

DAY EIGHTY-NINE

Dave Branon, Long, and Mart DeHaan, *Our Daily Bread,* © 2004 by RBC Ministries, Grand Rapids, MI. Reprinted by permission. All rights reserved.

Jean Nicolas Grou 1731-1803 was a Jesuit priest. His works are in the public domain.

DAY NINETY

Quote by Lancelot Andrewes taken from *Prayers for the Week: From the Private Devotions of Lancelot Andrewes.* 1843 Public Domain.

DAY NINETY-ONE

Bosch and Grandstaff, *Our Daily Bread,* © 2004 by RBC Ministries, Grand Rapids, MI. Reprinted by permission. All rights reserved.

DAY NINETY-THREE

David Roper, Haddon Robinson, and Dave Branon, *Our Daily Bread,* © 2004 by RBC Ministries, Grand Rapids, MI. Reprinted by permission. All rights reserved.

DAY ONE HUNDRED FOUR

Richard DeHaan, *Our Daily Bread,* © 2004 by RBC Ministries, Grand Rapids, MI. Reprinted by permission. All rights reserved.

DAY ONE HUNDRED FIVE

Dave Egner and Les Stobbe, *Our Daily Bread,* © 2004 by RBC Ministries, Grand Rapids, MI. Reprinted by permission. All rights reserved.

DAY ONE HUNDRED SIX

Berry, *Our Daily Bread,* © 2004 by RBC Ministries, Grand Rapids, MI. Reprinted by permission. All rights reserved.

DAY ONE HUNDRED EIGHT

Falling in Love With Jesus by Dee Brestin and Kathy Trocolli, © 2000, Thomas Nelson Inc., Nashville, TN. Reprinted by permission. All rights reserved.

DAY ONE-HUNDRED NINE

Anne Cetas, *Our Daily Bread,* © 2004 by RBC Ministries, Grand Rapids, MI. Reprinted by permission. All rights reserved.

Printed in the USA
CPSIA information can be obtained
at www.ICGtesting.com
LVHW040945270823
756411LV00006B/204